INTERESTING FACTS ABOUT INDIA

An Educational Country Travel Picture Book for Kids about History, Destination Places, Animals and Many More

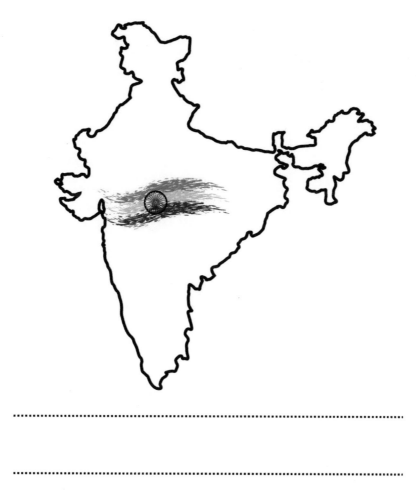

....

....

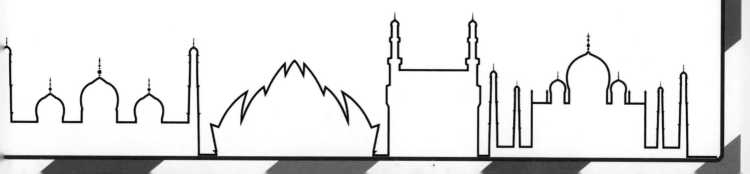

TABLE OF CONTENT

FACTS ABOUT INDIA'S GEOGRAPHY

India is the seventh-largest country in the world by land area, covering over 3 million square kilometres.

It is located in South Asia, bordered by Pakistan to the west, China and Nepal to the north, and Bangladesh and Myanmar to the east.

India is home to the Himalayan mountain range, the highest mountain range in the world. Mount Everest, the highest peak in the world, is located on the border between Nepal and China but is visible from parts of India.

The Thar Desert, also known as the Great Indian Desert, covers a large part of western India. It is the world's 17th largest desert and home to a variety of flora and fauna.

The Western Ghats mountain range runs along the western coast of India and is home to many species of plants and animals found nowhere else in the world.

- The country has a diverse climate, with hot and humid summers and mild winters in most parts. However, the northern region experiences extreme cold in the winter, and the western region is dry and hot in the summer.
- India has a long coastline, with the Arabian Sea to the west and the Bay of Bengal to the east. The country has many beaches, as well as a number of major ports.
- The country has abundant natural resources, including coal, iron ore, petroleum, and natural gas. It is also a major producer of tea, wheat, rice, and other agricultural products.
- The Ganges River, one of the holiest rivers in Hinduism, runs through northern India. It is also an important source of water for irrigation and hydroelectric power.
- India is home to a variety of ecosystems, including forests, grasslands, wetlands, and coral reefs. The country is home to many species of plants and animals, including the Bengal tiger, Asian elephant, and Indian rhinoceros.

FACTS ABOUT INDIA'S HISTORY

India has a long and varied history, with evidence of human habitation dating back to the Paleolithic period.

The Indus Valley Civilization, one of the oldest in the world, flourished in the region from 2500 BC to 1900 BC. The civilization was known for its sophisticated urban planning and water management systems.

India was ruled by a number of empires and dynasties over the centuries, including the Maurya, Gupta, and Mughal empires.

During the colonial period, India was ruled by the British East India Company and later the British Raj. The country gained independence in 1947 after a non-violent resistance movement led by Mahatma Gandhi.

India is a diverse country with a wide range of languages, religions, and cultural traditions. Hinduism is the dominant religion, but there are also significant populations of Muslims, Christians, and Buddhists.

FACTS ABOUT INDIA'S HISTORY

- The Indian subcontinent has a rich artistic and literary tradition, with a long history of poetry, drama, music, and dance.
- The Indian independence movement was influenced by a number of intellectuals and leaders, including Mahatma Gandhi, Jawaharlal Nehru, and B. R. Ambedkar.
- India has a federal parliamentary democratic republic form of government, with a president and a prime minister as the head of state and government, respectively.
- India has made significant economic and technological progress in recent years, and is now one of the world's fastest-growing economies.
- The country has a vibrant and diverse culture, with many festivals and traditions celebrated throughout the year. Some of the most well-known festivals include Diwali, Holi, and Navaratri.

FACTS ABOUT INDIA'S GOVERNMENT AND POLITICS

India is a federal parliamentary democratic republic with a president and a prime minister as heads of state and government, respectively.

The country has a bicameral parliament, with the upper house (Rajya Sabha) and the lower house (Lok Sabha).

The president is elected by an electoral college for a five-year term and is responsible for appointing the prime minister and other key government officials.

The prime minister is the head of government and is responsible for leading the executive branch of government and implementing the policies of the government.

India has a multi-party political system, with a number of national and regional parties vying for power. The two main national parties are the Bharatiya Janata Party (BJP) and the Indian National Congress (INC).

FACTS ABOUT INDIA'S GOVERNMENT AND POLITICS

- India has a vibrant civil society, with a wide range of non-governmental organization (NGOs) working on issues such as human rights, environmental conservation, and social justice.
- The country has a free and independent press, with many newspapers and television and radio stations operating across the country.
- India has a long history of peaceful and democratic elections, with universal suffrag for all citizens over the age of 18.
- The country has a complex legal system, with a mix of common law and civil law, a well as personal laws based on religious and cultural traditions.
- India's political climate is often marked by tension and polarization, with debates an controversies over issues such as religion, nationalism, and social justice.

FACTS ABOUT INDIA'S ECONOMY

India is the world's fifth-largest economy and one of the fastest-growing economies in the world.

The country has a mixed economy, with both the private and public sectors playing a significant role.

The service sector is the largest contributor to India's GDP, followed by industry and agriculture.

Major industries in India include IT and business process outsourcing, textiles and apparel, pharmaceuticals, and engineering.

India is the world's second-largest producer of wheat and rice and a major producer of a variety of other agricultural products, including sugarcane, cotton, and tea.

- The country is home to a number of major ports and is a major trading partner fo many countries around the world.
- India has a large and growing middle class, with increasing levels of consumption an investment.
- However, the country also faces significant challenges, including high levels of povert and inequality and a large informal sector.
- The government has implemented a number of economic reforms and developmen programmes in recent years, aimed at promoting growth and reducing poverty.
- India is a member of a number of regional and international economic organization including the World Trade Organization (WTO) and the South Asian Association fc Regional Cooperation (SAARC).

FACTS ABOUT INDIA'S SOCIETY AND CULTURE

- India is the second-most populous country in the world, with over 1.4 billion people.
- The country is home to a wide range of linguistic and ethnic groups, with more than 1,600 languages spoken. Hindi and English are the two official languages.
- Hinduism is the dominant religion in India, followed by Islam, Christianity, and other religions.
- India has a long and diverse cultural tradition, with a rich history of literature, music, dance, and visual arts.
- The country is known for its diverse cuisine, with a wide range of regional and local dishes influenced by different cultural and historical factors.

- India has a complex system of social hierarchy and a history of caste-based discrimination. However, the country has made significant progress in recent years in addressing issues of social inequality and discrimination.
- The family is an important unit of society in India, and joint family systems are common in many parts of the country.
- Education is highly valued in India, and the country has a large and growing literacy rate.
- India has a number of major festivals and cultural events, such as Diwali, Holi, and Navaratri, which are celebrated with great enthusiasm and fanfare.
- The country has a vibrant and diverse media landscape, with a wide range of television and radio stations, newspapers, and online platforms.

FACTS ABOUT INDIA'S SOCIETY AND CULTURE

- Education is a fundamental right in India, and the government provides free and compulsory education to children between the ages of 6 and 14.
- The country has a large and growing education system, with over 1.5 million schools and over 35,000 higher education institutions.
- The education system in India is divided into primary, secondary, and higher education.
- Primary and secondary education is provided by government-run schools as well as private schools. The curriculum is determined by the National Council for Educational Research and Training (NCERT).
- Higher education is provided by universities, colleges, and institutes, which offer a wide range of courses in a variety of disciplines.

- India has a number of prestigious universities and colleges, including the India Institutes of Technology (IITs) and the Indian Institutes of Management (IIMs), which are known for their high-quality education and research.
- The country has a large and growing number of international students, with man foreign universities setting up campuses in India.
- The education system in India faces a number of challenges, including low levels c literacy and high dropout rates in some areas.
- The government has implemented a number of initiatives and programmes to improv the quality and accessibility of education in the country.
- Education is highly valued in India, and parents and families place a strong emphas on the education and career prospects of their children.

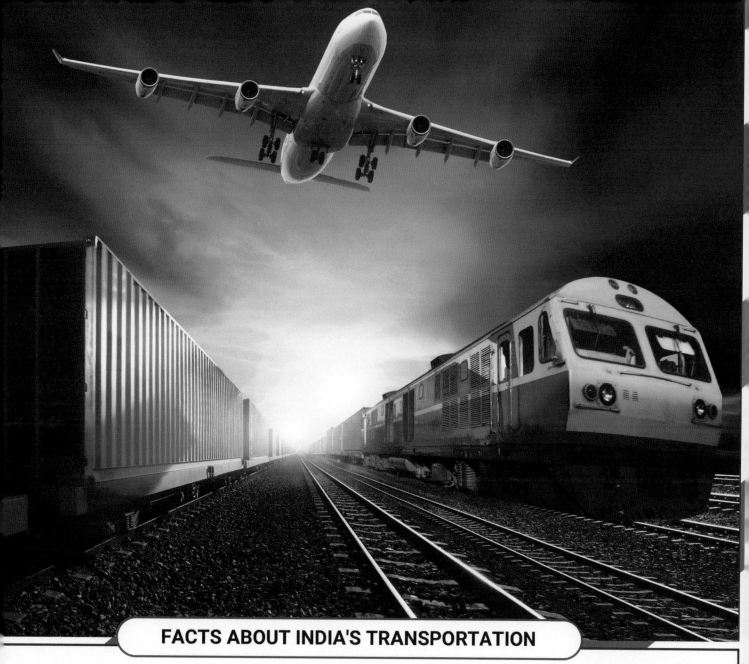

FACTS ABOUT INDIA'S TRANSPORTATION

- India has a vast and diverse transportation network, comprising roads, railways, airports, and waterways.
- The country has the second-largest road network in the world, with over 5.5 million kilometres of roads.
- The Indian Railways is the fourth-largest railway network in the world, with over 115,000 kilometres of track. It is the primary mode of long-distance travel in the country and also serves as a major freight carrier.
- India has a number of major airports, with the busiest being the Indira Gandhi International Airport in Delhi. The country has a growing domestic and international air travel market.
- The country also has a number of major ports, including the Jawaharlal Nehru Port in Mumbai, which is the busiest container port in India.

- In recent years, the government has made significant investments in improving and expanding the transportation infrastructure, including the construction of new roads, railways, and airports.
- India has a number of public transportation options, including buses, trains, and metro systems in major cities.
- The country also has a thriving taxi and ride-hailing market, with a number of local and international companies operating in the country.
- India has a number of domestic and international shipping companies and is a major hub for shipping and logistics in the region.
- Transportation in India can be challenging due to a combination of crowded roads, inadequate infrastructure, and traffic congestion in major cities.

FACTS ABOUT INDIA'S FOOD AND CUISINE

- Indian cuisine is known for its diverse and flavorful dishes, made with a wide range of ingredients and cooking techniques.
- Indian food is influenced by a number of factors, including regional and local traditions, cultural and historical influences, and climate and geography.
- Indian cuisine is characterised by the use of a variety of spices, including cumin, turmeric, coriander, and cardamom.
- Rice and wheat are the staple grains in India and are used in a variety of dishes, including rice pilaf, roti, and naan.
- Indian cuisine includes a wide range of vegetarian and non-vegetarian dishes, and there is a significant tradition of vegetarianism in many parts of the country.

- Popular Indian dishes include curry, biryani, tandoori chicken, and dal makhani.
- Indian cuisine is known for its sweet dishes, including gulab jamun, ras malai, and kulfi.
- Tea is a popular beverage in India, and the country is one of the largest producers of tea in the world.
- Indian food is often served with a variety of side dishes and condiments, including chutneys, pickles, and raita.
- Indian cuisine has a global presence, with Indian restaurants and dishes found in many countries around the world.

FACTS ABOUT INDIA'S ARTS AND ENTERTAINMENT

- India has a long and diverse tradition of art and culture, with a wide range of artistic and literary forms.
- The country has a rich history of literature, with a number of ancient and modern works in a variety of languages.
- Indian music is diverse and varied, with a number of classical and folk traditions, as well as popular and contemporary genres.
- Indian cinema, also known as Bollywood, is one of the largest and most popular film industries in the world.
- The country has a thriving theater scene, with a number of professional and amateur companies staging a wide range of plays and musicals.

- Indian art encompasses a wide range of styles and media, including painting, sculpture, and architecture.
- The country has a number of major art museums and galleries, as well as a thriving contemporary art scene.
- India is home to a number of major cultural festivals and events, including the Kumbh Mela, a massive Hindu pilgrimage, and the International Film Festival of India.
- Indian popular culture is diverse and dynamic, with a range of music, television, and social media trends influencing young people in the country.
- India has a vibrant and diverse media landscape, with a range of television and radio stations, newspapers, and online platforms catering to different audiences and interests.

LANDMARKS AND TOURIST ATTRACTIONS

- India is home to a number of iconic landmarks and tourist attractions, including the Taj Mahal, the Red Fort, and the Gateway of India.
- The Taj Mahal, located in Agra, is a UNESCO World Heritage Site and one of the most visited tourist attractions in the world. It is a white marble mausoleum built in the 17th century as a tribute to the Mughal Emperor Shah Jahan's wife.

LANDMARKS AND TOURIST ATTRACTIONS

- The Red Fort, also located in Agra, is a historic fort complex that was the main residence of the Mughal emperors. It is now a popular tourist destination, and a symbol of India's struggle for independence.

- The Gateway of India, located in Mumbai, is a iconic archway that was built to commemorate the visit of King George V and Queen Mary in 1911. It is a popular tourist destination and a symbol of the city.

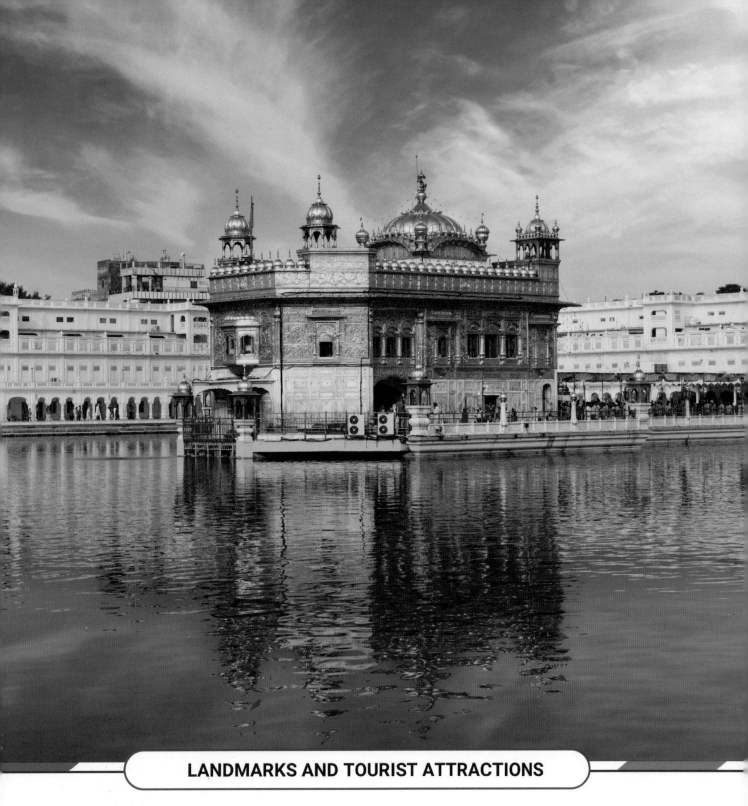

LANDMARKS AND TOURIST ATTRACTIONS

- India is home to a number of major temples and religious sites, including the Golden Temple in Amritsar, the Vaishno Devi Temple in Jammu, and the Meenakshi Temple in Madurai.
- The country has a number of beautiful beaches, including Goa, a popular tourist destination known for its sand, sun, and nightlife.

LANDMARKS AND TOURIST ATTRACTIONS

- India is home to a number of national parks and wildlife reserves, including the Kaziranga National Park in Assam, which is home to the one-horned rhinoceros.
- The country has a number of mountain ranges and hill stations, including the Himalayas, which are popular destinations for trekking and adventure sports.

LANDMARKS AND TOURIST ATTRACTIONS

- India has a rich history and cultural heritage, and a number of historical sites and landmarks, including the Agra Fort, the Qutub Minar, and the Ellora Caves.
- The country has a number of major festivals and events that attract tourists from around the world, including the Pushkar Camel Fair, the Kumbh Mela, and the Holi Festival of Colors.

LANDMARKS AND TOURIST ATTRACTIONS

- India is home to a diverse range of animal species, including mammals, birds, reptiles, and amphibians.
- The country has a number of national parks and wildlife reserves, which provide habitat and protection for a wide range of species.
- India is home to a number of iconic and endangered species, including the Bengal tiger, the Indian elephant, and the one-horned rhinoceros.

LANDMARKS AND TOURIST ATTRACTIONS

- The Bengal tiger is the national animal of India, and is found in a number of national parks, including the Sundarbans National Park in West Bengal.
- The Indian elephant is found in a number of national parks and reserves, and is an important cultural and religious symbol in the country.
- The one-horned rhinoceros is found in the Kaziranga National Park in Assam, and is a critically endangered species.

LANDMARKS AND TOURIST ATTRACTIONS

- India is home to a number of species of primates, including the bonobo, the gibbon, and the macaque.
- The country is also home to a wide range of bird species, including the national bird, the Indian peafowl, and the critically endangered great Indian bustard.

LANDMARKS AND TOURIST ATTRACTIONS

- India has a number of reptiles, including snakes, lizards, and crocodilians. The country is home to the Bengal monitor, a large reptile found in the Western Ghats.
- The country has a number of amphibians, including the Indian purple frog, which is found in the Western Ghats and is known for its distinctive appearance and secretive habits.

FACTS ABOUT INDIA'S SPORTS

- Cricket is the most popular sport in India, and the Indian national team is one of the top-ranked teams in the world.

- India has a professional cricket league, the Indian Premier League (IPL), which is one of the most successful and popular sports leagues in the world.

- Field hockey is the national sport of India, and the Indian national team has won eight Olympic gold medals in the sport.

- Football is also popular in India, and the Indian Super League (ISL) is the top professional league in the country.

- Tennis is another popular sport in India, with a number of top players, including Sania Mirza and Mahesh Bhupathi, competing at the international level.

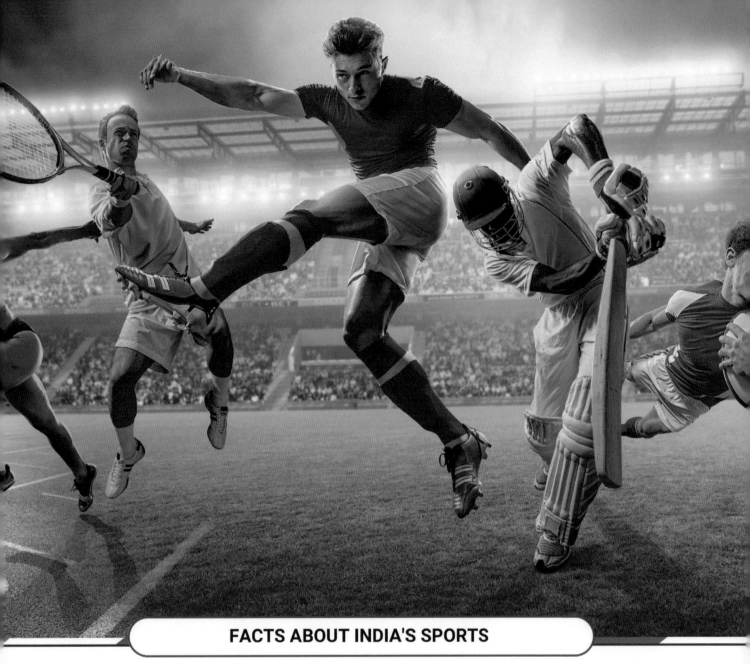

FACTS ABOUT INDIA'S SPORTS

- The country has a number of major sports facilities and venues, including the Jawaharlal Nehru Stadium in Delhi and the Wankhede Stadium in Mumbai.
- India has a strong tradition in Olympic sports, and has won a number of medals in sports such as wrestling, boxing, and weightlifting.
- The country is also home to a number of adventure sports, such as trekking, rafting, and paragliding.
- The Indian Olympic Association is the national Olympic committee for India, and is responsible for representing the country at the Olympic Games.
- India has a number of major sports events and tournaments, including the Indian Open golf tournament and the Indian Grand Prix, a round of the Formula One World Championship.

FACTS ABOUT INDIA'S ARMY

- The Indian Army is the land-based branch of the Indian Armed Forces, and is responsible for defending the country's borders and maintaining internal security.
- The Indian Army is one of the largest armies in the world, with over 1.4 million active personnel.
- The army is organized into a number of corps and divisions, which are responsible for different areas of operations.
- The Indian Army has a number of specialized units, including the Parachute Regiment, the Special Forces, and the Military Police.
- The Indian Army has a number of major equipment and weapons systems, including tanks, artillery, and aircraft.

FACTS ABOUT INDIA'S ARMY

- The army has a long and distinguished history, and has played a significant role in India's independence struggle and in maintaining regional stability.
- The Indian Army has participated in a number of peacekeeping missions around the world, and is a member of the United Nations peacekeeping force.
- The army is headed by the Chief of Army Staff, who is responsible for the overall command and control of the force.
- The Indian Army has a number of training institutes and academies, including the Indian Military Academy, the National Defense Academy, and the Indian Naval Academy.
- The Indian Army is a volunteer force, and soldiers are recruited from across the country through a competitive examination process.

Printed in Great Britain
by Amazon

16580595R00020